A Jesuit Trained Jewish Doctor from the St. Louis Ghetto Shares NEW MESSAGES FROM GOD

A Jesuit Trained Jewish Doctor from the St. Louis Ghetto Shares NEW MESSAGES FROM GOD

By Edward O. Bierman, M.D.

Press
Los Angeles, CA.

A JESUIT TRAINED JEWISH DOCTOR FROM THE ST. LOUIS GHETTO SHARES NEW MESSAGES FROM GOD

Third Edition ISBN 978-1-105-95417-7

Chapters

FOREWORD

The events described in this book began with a revelation from God. It changed the course of my life, and affected my entire family. In addition to my wife Shirley and our children, three persons were very important in the course of the events that followed. Father Francis J. Parrish, S.J., who for over forty years acted as a spiritual guide, mentor, and big brother, was in constant touch with me. Dr. Edward Colbert, M.D., a psychiatrist and prominent Catholic layperson, was very helpful in introducing me to organizations and groups that enabled me to share the messages with others. Dr. Colbert and I were very good friends; ours was not a doctor-patient relationship. Dr. Otto Lobstein, Ph.D., introduced me to his research. This led to my research with lysozyme, in human beings, including my own cancer. Our efforts met with considerable success, and with very powerful resistance. This book is a partial story of a very long journey. It is my hope and prayer that you find it interesting and helpful.

Chapter One

REVELATION

It was a beautiful evening in Pacific Palisades. In the land of perpetual springtime, this was not at all unusual. As it says in fairy tales, the children (and their mothers) were safely tucked away in their beds.

For over three years it had been my habit to study the books of the New Testament and collateral literature at night, when all was still. If I was too tired to do so and went to sleep, I would be awakened and in a refreshed state. Then I could pursue the study properly. I had completed over three years of study. The hour study period was divided into three parts; first, a period of reading. Second, a time for thinking about what I had read. Third, a period of what I called Godtemplation. In this period, I would leave my mind free and permit it and God to do with it as He wished. This final exercise would leave me relaxed and ready for sleep.

It was close to twelve o'clock, midnight, the temperature was very comfortable. All was very still. I was very sleepy having completed a hard day at the office, helped get the children off to bed, and completed my studies. Slumped across my barrel-shaped living room chair, my eyes half closed, I heard or felt an inner voice. I sensed a presence in the room, in front and to the left of me about ten feet away. It conveyed this message, "The Russians will be converted." I promptly responded, "What do you want for it?" He answered, "A sacrifice without waste."

I rose from the chair and found a scrap of paper on the floor. Striking a match, I lit the paper and threw it into the fireplace. I asked, "Like this?" He answered, "On that order."

I suddenly realized that I was not dreaming. I began to shake, tremble and experience extreme discomfort. Christ had communicated with me. I felt a second presence in the room, close to me and on my right side. Spontaneously I spoke out in a voice full of emotion, "Mary, make him stop." There was no further communication.

I sat there, clothed only in my underwear, considering what had occurred. Would Jesus talk to a man in his underwear? Would Mary be present in such a time? What happened?

The night was still, quiet, and comfortable. The room was filled with comfortable furniture: a piano, a fireplace, which was unused that evening, and a small bar, also unused. My wife and children were resting quietly in their beds. I alone had changed, and would never again be the same. Thoughts raced through my mind in wild order. What was this? I saw nothing, heard nothing; the experience was purely internal. Yet, there was a sense of presence of two beings outside of me. I had spoken to them. I had struck a match and ignited a piece of paper. It was no dream. So what else should I do? After proper preparation, I got close to my wife and went to sleep.

The next morning was another beautiful day. The sun filtered through the leaves of the giant three hundred year old oak tree that sheltered our bedroom. I did all the usual chores; breakfast, helping get the children ready, goodbye kisses, and then was off to the office. I drove my 190 Mercedes Benz a block south on Bienveneda to the famous Sunset Boulevard, turned left, followed the street past the synagogue and churches, the quaint Palisades Village, turned right and drove down Chautauqua.

Chautauqua is a beautiful road leading from Sunset to the Pacific Coast Highway at Will Rogers' Beach and the Pacific Ocean. Magnificent homes and gardens, well kept and loved, line the road as it gently curves to the ocean. At the meeting point of the highway and the road, a mansion hangs on the edge of the cliff. For over forty years it has threatened to fall on the highway. Perhaps this is a symbol of the area; living high, beautifully and dangerously, most snug and protected from others. A sharp turn left and up Channel to Seventh Street into the then small city of Santa Monica, then again gently downward to Wilshire Boulevard. I daily passed the Santa Monica Catholic Church, with its beautiful statue of Mary. Occasionally, I would stop and pray. The tree line on the street gave a feeling of comfort and protection as they arched over, forming a green canopy. The sun was up on a friendly sky and a calm world. The events of the previous night were filed away for future reference and forgotten, as just an aberration of some type. Yet, all these places and things were to take part in a deepening series of events, which would involve me in conflict with doctrine of the Catholic Church, the policies of the federal government, the Federal Drug Administration, and in world events including the major powers of China, Russia, and most especially with Israel.

I spent the day in my office, seeing and treating patients for diseases of the eye. It was a wonderful place to work. Dr. Marvin Mack, the very image of the title Doctor of the T.V. show Dr. Willoughby, owned and worked from this building. Dr. Mack was Catholic and prominent in the area. He was an excellent family physician. He was my physician and advisor. Intelligent, experienced, with mid-Western farmer's ethics, he was a man who exemplified good medicine and good business sense. The only complaint I ever heard against him was that his fees were too high. He responded by saying that he did not have to see his patients as often because he gave them more time per visit and had to charge accordingly. He felt that this was greater economy and resulted in getting the patient back to his or her occupation more quickly. Marvin had a series of young assistants working for him just as did the doctor who appeared on the T.V. series. He worked at St. John's Hospital and Santa Monica Hospital. St. John's was the hospital pictured in the series. It was a storybook place...Hollywood stories.

The building's physicians' area was one story, with a unique air-conditioning system. It used the cool fresh air coming from the westerly breeze off the Pacific Ocean.

The parking lot was free to the doctors. The patients' parking lot was also free. The waiting room was appointed for adults in one area and children in another. The two areas were separated by a wall which contained a beautiful aquarium. A beautiful warm fireplace for cool days completed the picture. Rest facilities were available. The waiting room served five physicians, and it was quite large. It faced the business office.

The working conditions were excellent. The other doctors had their front office staff there. The hall led right and left, to offices on either side. Dr. William Linton and Dr. Mack were in the south wing. Dr. Jack Rooney and I were in the north wing. The office was tastefully decorated in earth tones and very efficiently furnished. Back stations were available for nursing help.

I had converted a treatment room into an office for my secretary, Evelyn Andrews. I had the other treatment room. A large refracting lane, office and study combination and a comfortable room in which the patients could wait while their pupils dilated, completed the suite. The suite was built on to the existing structure with my modifications.

Joint facilities included a family-like room where we all took coffee and lunch. There was a large room for minor surgery, an X-ray department, pharmacy, and a laboratory.

It was a dream of a set-up. It was one big happy family, as far as I was concerned, for about fifteen years.

At night I would drive home. Sometimes I would take the California incline down to the Pacific Coast Highway and watch the sun set on the Pacific, before starting up Chautauqua to Sunset Boulevard. I turned into my carport situated at the very foot of the Santa Monica Mountains and looked at the beauty of the hills in which we were nestled.

Occasionally, I glanced at the storm drain next to our driveway. It would serve as a nuclear shelter in case of an attack, as far as I was concerned. It was deep, roomy, and had access to many areas. The hills around our home provided as much protection as would be available.

I went in to the house to be greeted by my beautiful, busy wife, the five children, and our collie dog. Our collie, Princess, considered herself a true member of the family. If I didn't pet her quickly enough she would nibble on my thigh, a painful way to get my attention. It was very effective communication, and one I did not forget, I couldn't.

Dinner, discussions and at times, discipline, were the order of the evening. With five children there was always something going on: some fun, some drama, some illness or oftentimes, a new or injured pet brought home for me to, "make (her/him) better, Daddy." The love and confidence in my ability as a doctor was appreciated, but the reality of life and death presented to me in some of these cases proved as ever, to be in God's hands. Nature and God ...ever present lessons in life.

After dinner, sometimes during dinner, we played a game at the table. We brought a "Menu Tree" mural design from our Army days at Ft. Leonard Wood in Missouri. We painted it on the kitchen wall. It was a colorfully painted tree with fruits, vegetables, meats, and so on. The game was for one of us to select an object, and mentally project the thought to others. It was fun. It was quiet, and I hoped that it would sharpen the extrasensory perception of the children. Maybe it sharpened mine as well. It brought peace to the table. It brought a listening for something within. We discussed the problems the children had for the day or anything anyone brought up.

One of the questions was why didn't I plant a tree like that; I wouldn't have to work so hard. I had to explain that it was a good idea, but that such trees simply did not exist. Little did I know that I would be involved in planting trees very shortly.

After Shirley and the children were asleep, I went into the living room to study. I had put the events of the previous night in the back of my mind. I was relaxed and comfortable.

I started to read the chapter of the New Testament I had selected. This particular book had been given to my by Father Klyber, a converted Jew, now a priest in 1944. It was inscribed, "To my friend Ed Bierman. May the voice of the long desired Messiah speak to you from these remarkable pages. God bless you. Father Klyber".

He had. I had everything I wanted. I had my family, a wonderful wife and five great children, my collie, a good office, research projects, and men to help me with my work, adequate income, and peace and quiet. Thoughtfully contented, I started to study. I continued for a few lines, and looked up. A presence, a tall well-built man approached from the dark dining room toward me. He stood about ten feet away, a vague outline. He spoke softly within me. "Ed, I want you..." I didn't wait to hear the words. I jumped to my feet, infuriated at the interruption, frightened by the presence. "Who are you to tell me what to do?" I demanded within myself. I turned my back on the presence and started to walk away. Even as I did so, I could see his features vaguely in my mind's eye. He answered me in a voice so gentle and a manner so benignly sweet, that I was calmed. "I am the Messiah, Ed." I knew the voice. I had experienced it before, but not with the presence. Not like this. It had done many things in my life, for me. It had brought me to experiment with lysozyme in the treatment of cancer. This voice, since my youth, had nurtured and protected me, but he had never identified himself so clearly. "Then the drug for Lysozyme will work." I replied a lot more respectfully. This was no ordinary being or ghost. This was the "Boss" if he were true. I felt that I had made a bargain that was "good" for my fellow man. If this drug would help people with cancer, what a boon it would be.

He nodded, YES. We had a deal. Then I asked, "Please put your messages in a dream. I cannot stand this, it is too much."

Fear of the presence and its power made me believe that dreaming would be easier; I would not have to doubt my sanity. So I thought. Well, live and learn.

Chapter Two

RESEARCH

The year was 1959, in what was to be known as the golden years of medicine. We had just won two wars to defend freedom, and we were to a large degree, free. Free to study. Free to experiment. Free to try new things, new ideas, and new drugs. Nature had made a mix of human beings from foreign lands with fresh ideas, departed from the old customs and concepts. We were like children, tasting, feeling, standing, falling, always trying, always trying.

At a party in the Pacific Palisades at the home of Dr. Earl and Bernadyne Holzman, I met Dr. Otto Lobstein. Otto was a European Jew who fled to England to escape the Nazi onslaught. In England he was interred as a citizen of an enemy nation. There, in prison camp, the internees established classes and studied. After that war, he came to Northwestern University and studied the enzyme Lysozyme. His studies focused first, on Lysozyme as a part of the defense system of the body, later, at the University of Southern California as a drug to treat experimental malignancy in mice. He and his partner Dr. Sol Dulkin established a biochemical laboratory, in Beverly Hills. Their last research went unpublished. Economically, they did well.

I loved research. I started doing research playing with ants as a child. I watched them solve problems that I set before them; I watched them go to war with one another. I observed rats fighting our pigeons, and in turn our dogs hunting them. I played with our horse, Bill. I tried pulling his wagon, breaking his rope.

My father, Dr. Max John Bierman, was a family practitioner. As a student, on scholarship at Washington University, he had suggested a method of visualizing the gall bladder through the use of X-rays and dyes. He was proud that the idea was taken up by someone and proved to be true. Thus, he inspired me to do likewise. It was simply applying a childish desire to learn, to an adult desire to do so under regulated conditions.

In my internship at St. Mary's group of hospitals at St. Louis University, I followed in my father's footsteps. Thanks to my friend, Dr. Charles Cherre, I found myself on the "chronic disease" side of the medical floor. It was quiet. One of my patients had emphysema. I asked permission to try physiotherapy. It was granted. After ten days of exercises and massage, my patient declared himself cured and capable of directing his own physiotherapist. "Go forth and do others," he directed. I wrote up the treatment and noted that asthmatics in Israel were receiving similar therapy. The concept was adopted by the medical department for investigation. I had followed my dad's lead. I did not get to follow this idea; it was done for me.

In my first six months of residency in eye diseases, I took an idea away from the lunch table. Dr. Dallas Dyer had just finished a study in electroencephalography, and we all wondered what it would show in amblyopia, commonly called a "lazy eye." The other residents were too occupied, so I studied it after obtaining permission from my superiors. It happened that a large percentage showed abnormal brain waves. The study pointed to the brain as the source of the problem. This time Dr. Leslie Drews insisted that I take credit, present the data, and publish it.

At this time, married, with one child and another on the way, I joined the Army residency-training program. When called into service, I continued to do research, publish, study, and advance medically during the time of the Korean action.

I enjoyed all of my Army service with the exception of one hour. All my regular superiors were kind, helpful, and understanding. One day, I had a temporary substitute commanding officer; we had a brief difference of opinion.

When the Korean War entered the discussion phase, I resigned my commission. At that time, the Army had renewed its offer of a year of training for a year of service. I had served my time. Now we had three children, and one on the way. It was time to go. The Army life is very difficult on children of school age and their parents.

After discharge from the Army, we moved to Los Angeles, California. In this gigantic city, we found our home in the Pacific Palisades. It was what we dreamed of having. Morning sun, evening sun, the mountains and the ocean breeze... a perfect picture. We had a small home in St. Louis, which we sold. It was at 1932 Vinita; we moved to 913 Bienveneda. Good welcome. With the assistance from both of our families, a trusting builder, a friendly bank, and a guiding Spirit, we embarked on what I hoped would be a peaceful, calm life.

I took a job with Ross-Loos medical clinic, when my offer from a private doctor collapsed. It was to be a wonderful experience. I worked with other doctors, from other residencies, and with one older doctor who had retired from Chicago. There was a good deal of medicine and surgery to do. As it was all pre-paid, there was practically no hassle. I continued to study. I obtained my "boards." I began private practice.

I met Dr. Louis Jaques, one of the world's leading optometrists. We became fast friends. He helped me and taught me a considerable amount of refraction and muscle balance. He also was a complete gentleman. He loved his patients and that is the way he healed them. That element was not in his reports.

I established a private practice. I then took over the practice of Dr. Kinney who was ill. On his death, I purchased what was left of it, for in two years it had become mostly mine. Joined with my own, it was adequate to go on my own. I resigned from Ross-Loos. I couldn't get an appointment at UCLA. I was advised to start my own research group. And so I did, with Shirley's encouragement. She felt UCLA was not for me.

Otto and I brought many people together, brainstormed the ideas and then created the Research Foundation for Diseases of the Eye, and its goals. We had enough research ideas. We needed a group to help fund them and to establish a presentable base for operations. We were to seek funds in the way of grants and donations. We planned to work at Redlands University, in the Beverly Hills laboratory, and at medical offices for clinical work. Naturally things did not go as planned. So it always was to be.

Our first donation was from Mr. Hyman Fox, my father-in-law. He gave us fifteen hundred dollars to start, after I explained what we were going to try to do. We accepted it as a loan, hoping to be funded through other private corporate, or government channels; both rejected us.

We were told that government grants would go to medical schools. Grants were to be based more on the government's desire to control the medical schools than on the value of the research. We were told, in effect, not to waste our time. It was sound advice, but Otto, with University backing, continued from time to time, to apply for grants from both sources...with negative results.

The clinical work at Redlands on the effect of Lysozyme in ointment form on acne languished. The research into the basic science of the clarity of the crystalline lens went forward with our grant to a student who created a machine to study it. With his device, he attempted to maintain the clarity of the lens, separated from the eye, in various solutions over time.

I picked up the work on skin lesions, and found that Lysozyme did decrease lesions in acne. Our pharmacist, Mr. Charles Hamilton, in Dr. Mack's building, made the ointment. I tried it on ten patients with some good results. Then a strange thing happened to me one day on my way to the laboratory. I was driving my car and thinking about the work I would do with lenses. In a completely relaxed state, something within me said, "Why don't you cure cancer first?" As if a small doll-like person within my abdomen had given me the word.

When I got to the laboratory, I began to discuss my research plans with Otto. I informed him that it was strange that a cancer had never been found in a human lens. He answered, matter-of-factly, that it was probably because the lens was bathed in Lysozyme. (It isn't. But because of the strange occurrence a short time before, I did not interrupt him.) He said that he and Sol had done experiments treating CH3 mice with Gardner's lymphosarcoma, a one hundred percent fatal experimental cancer in mice, with Lysozyme. Some mice survived, some had prolonged life spans, and the offspring of the survivors were resistant to implantation with malignancy. This work was observed and commented upon by Dr. Edward Dousy, a respected pathologist.

I was shocked when Otto brought the old unpublished article out of his desk drawer. I took it home at night and read it. It convinced me that the drug had been effective and that it was worthy of trial in human beings, especially because it was not toxic. The disease on the other hand, was fatal.

Otto had received a request from Dr. Rudolpho Ferrari for any new article on Lysozyme for a symposium in Milan, Italy. He asked what I thought. Twenty-seven rejections had made him cautious. I suggested that he change the title of the article from, "Lysozyme in Malignancy" to "Lysozyme in the treatment of CH3 Mice with Gardner's Lymphosarcoma". This was more correct, and less sensational. Secondly, I suggested that he submit the article using the name of the foundation, and say that I had submitted, but not authored it. Hopefully, it would add to its credibility.

Otto was elated when the article was accepted. He went to Milan to the meeting. He returned with the news that Lysozyme was now being used in Italy to treat the pain caused by cancer, but not for a long period. No one had yet tried to suppress the cancer, but over a twenty day period eighty percent of the patients had less pain and difficulty. He had been received like a hero and treated with great respect. It was not only for this work, but also for the greater body of research he had done on this enzyme. Years of study had been fruitful.

I became determined to complete the work. To my scientific mind, it was a wonderful thing to do for humanity. If we made a cheap, non-toxic drug for cancer, what a gift to mankind it would be. Now I had the Revelation, so my spiritual side was screaming to do it. I had that "gut" sensation on the way to the laboratory, so my gambling instinct was for it. The combination of everything in me said, "Go for it."

With all of this, I still could and did not believe it. It was literally too good to be true, but we had to prove or disprove it. That's research. Now there were two questions I wanted answered. Not only does Lysozyme work, but also, does God communicate this way?

Chapter Three

DREAMS, ETC. ETC.

When I requested that the "Boss" put his messages in a dream form, I thought it would be much easier. I was wrong, and I was soon to modify my request to, do what you want, but take it easy on me.

I had had ESP experiences before. The first, at age four when my grandfather's horse caught my eye and somehow I knew that he was thirsty. The dogs and Bill, the horse, had no difficulty in getting me to do things for them. As childhood playmates, opening the door to the kitchen was the first trick they taught me. All they wanted me to do was to let them get to grandmother, Baba. Getting petted was easy. Bill used charades also. His head dipping into the manger where hay was placed was his signal for hay. The oat box was another easy one. Getting his stall cleaned was accomplished by stamping his feet. During this time, my parents and grandparents were very supportive. Baba always backed me up in the food department for the dogs. Grandpa was the one who had to clean the stall and give permission for oats for Bill. He gave me a lecture on the amount of oats to give Bill. With the half can of oats, Bill got a lecture from me on not eating too much. Hay was an item that he could have at any time in moderate amounts.

When I first heard that I was playing with "dumb animals," I told the problem to my dad. "They are not dumb," I said. "That doesn't mean they are stupid," my father replied, "it only means that they cannot speak."

Okay, they couldn't speak, but they could certainly know what they wanted me to do, and how to get me to do it.

When Bill communicated his thirst telepathically with a constant stare, I climbed down the back steps, filled a bucket with water, and started for the stable. This was extremely difficult for me. I needed both hands to lift the bucket. Bill saw my problem immediately. With one movement of his head, he pulled himself free from his stall and met me in the yard. The way he drained that bucket sent me to get the hose, and run it to the bucket. When he had his fill, I led him back to the stall, noticing the thick, heavy rope and the six-by-six wood post from which Bill had pulled it free. For the first time I realized how strong he was and what he could have done to me all the years we were together. He had never so much as flicked me with his tail.

I was soon to go to Hebrew school and learn that God communicated with the Prophets. I had no problem with that. If Bill could do it with me, so could they with God!

I continued my studies. Now in my thirties, I had incorporated baptism with prayers when I prepared for bed. I asked, "Whom do you wish me to contact about this?" That night I saw in a dream the northern approach to Loyola University as seen from Lincoln Boulevard. In that dream, I zoomed in on a black robed Jesuit at the university. "These are your Brothers," the voice announced.

This seemed entirely logical since the Jesuits had trained me. After graduating Beaumont High School, I entered St. Louis University, midterm January 1940. I was the only Hebrew in my class. Father Martin, the assistant dean, directed me to a Jewish senior on the school newspaper. The senior made it clear that he was too busy to be of any assistance to me. I wandered around the school trying to orient myself from the basement to the highest stacks of the library, from north to south.

At the north end, I came to a door I had never previously opened that especially attracted me. When I touched the knob, a voice within me said, "Welcome, Ed." I would never feel alone at school again. Always welcome. I entered the chapel I had never seen or dreamed of such overwhelming beauty. The lights gave the walls a golden hue, and there were golden objects of religious art. The stained glass windows admitted light that transformed the room into a glimpse of heaven.

This Jewish boy had never seen anything like it. The air was filled with the aroma of incense, and though I may not have known it at the time, the presence of a warm, loving, protective, comforting spirit of brothers and sisters and, I believe, God.

I would return often for prayer, rest, re-energizing and contemplation. I was invited by a classmate to attend mass. I was happy to oblige. It was beautiful and interesting and I followed the English translation of the Latin. I was surprised that a very good part of the prayers were identical to those I learned in Hebrew school. "Holy, Holy, Holy God of power and might, the whole world is full of your Glory." This short, clear praise of God especially moved me. I did it in Hebrew.

I became a regular attendant at Friday mass. I noticed I seemed to enjoy it more than the Catholic students. It seemed to put many to sleep and it seemed to have no affect on others. One Friday in the lounge, I sat near four classmates who were planning their Saturday night date. They were giving out the duties. This man would get a car, the next get the liquor to "loosen up the girls." The time came for mass. We all departed, and when mass was over, we returned to our previous seats. With absolute recall, as if nothing had happened, the men continued their plans. There seemed to be a complete separation between what was taught, and any idea of it being a basis for action.

I released myself completely at mass. I could see, and hear, and enjoy what was going on around me. However, I was in a reverie, a dreamlike contemplation, which gradually became more and more pleasant. Then something happened that I had never heard, or read. My soul seemed to leave my body and float upward. Gradually, on repeat visits, it went higher and higher until finally it reached the ceiling. I could see a density, and it could see me.

As mass ended, I felt that my body and soul were reunited; I returned refreshed and enthused to do my assignments.

The members of the class and my superiors noted my behavior. One day, one of my classmates requested that I go to mass and sign in for him. He offered me twenty-five cents to do so. I was suspicious. Did one of the Fathers put him up to it? Why ask me? Why not ask another classmate to sign twice? It was common practice. What could I say when requested to do this by a classmate who, "needed the time to study" for a test? If I refused, I would be considered a nerd.

I told him to put the money in the poor box, and promise to go to mass Sunday. He did, and I did, and I never saw or heard from him again.

Father Alphonse Schwitalla finally informed me in a letter what had happened to me at mass. This came many years later. He called it a controlled ecstasy. Father Schwitalla was dean of St. Louis University Medical School, and had occasion to hold mass at retreats for the students. We were friends. I attended, and he observed me.

Father Schwitalla and my dad were political adversaries in the medical field of politics. Dad represented the family practice physicians as head to the medical ethics committee of the St. Louis Medical Association. As dean of the medical school, Father Schwitalla controlled more votes, and won. However, in retrospect, medicine lost. The profession was split between the haves and the have-less, and was never to be joined against other adversaries of medicine. Dad wanted me to be a physician and asked if I could one day be accepted at St. Louis University. Father Schwitalla responded, "Yes, if he has the grades." These two men, who together fashioned me, were tough on the outside. It was an appearance they used to protect the soft inside, like the shell of a turtle. I knew when I dealt with them that they would put up a stern front. Sometimes it seemed that they made the way unnecessarily difficult, but I knew that they would die for me if need be. So it was that my father turned me over to the Jesuits to, "make a man out of me." Jesuits define "a man" differently than most.

Additional dreams followed in short order. I was in a room, at the end of which was a large picture window. On the right side of the room, between the window and me was Whistler's Mother, rocking chair and all. Behind the picture window, almost against it was a huge face. It was the face of Jim Brown the football player, now a man I would call a social activist on the way to sainthood. His eyes, however, were those of an Asian Pacific Islander. "I am not dead," the voice within said. I wet the bed in fear. Thank God for the mother in the dream; it somewhat lessened the intensity of my fear.

At that time, the post- holocaust "God is dead" theory was not being promulgated. But the denial of its rectitude came before it had been uttered as far as I was concerned.

The next dream was stranger still. I was under the belly of a large insect, a cockroach. Looking upwards from this position I could see the face of God in the clouds. The disapproving eyes held my gaze. This dream also had a severe frightening effect. I came away from it with knowledge of where we stood vis-`a-vis God.

That was it for me, as far as telling God how to send a message. No more frightening experiences occurred.

In my prayers I asked God to send his messages as he wished, but to take it easy on me. He proved too much for me. My prayer was answered and revelation followed quickly. It occurred frequently when I was driving. One day I asked, "What was the sacrifice without waste?" The answer came in one word, "PRIDE." Of course, a man would die for his precious pride. But of what tangible good was it? All the pride in the world would not buy or get you a cup of coffee or a donut. We have to admit that God knows best, and we are not wise animals, but stupid ones without him. It is that pride which is an affront to God.

Another beautiful day, driving down Chautauqua to the sea, I was thinking about the Trinity. "How could there be a committee, God?" I wondered. The voice was in me, the presence behind me. "Look at the hood," it said. I looked up and saw the symbol of the Mercedes. In a flash, I had it. Of course. It was one symbol with three elements. I worked it out this way: the circle represented God. The circle has no beginning and no end; it can be as large as the universe or small as a pinhead. A horizontal diameter represents the Holy Spirit. A line from the center of the circle, perpendicular to the diameter, a radius represents the Messiah. Thus, the three persons of the Trinity are represented in one symbol.

The intact symbol thus represented the universe, spanned by the Holy Spirit, under the law of the Christ. That law simply stated is "Be (good, kind) to your brothers and sisters." In Hebrew, one word covers both words and means more. "Tzedarvka" means justice, love, goodness and kindness. I did not know that word when I received the original message at age eighteen or so. At the time, I thought this concept only included immediate family; I came to realize it included all mankind, animals and environment.

Now with the explanation of the Trinity, using a symbol that children could understand, I was ready for the Jesuits. They believed that only God could reveal a comprehensible explanation. There were no parts of the symbol. It was one. A compound made up of elements, but distinctly one. If any elements were removed, it lost its meaning. It could be a circle, a dash, a one, a T, the Diner's club symbol. All together, it had a different meaning. Later, I learned through the gift of a Holy Spirit medal from a Catholic patient, that it was the symbol used by the first century "Christians." I had to research the medal's symbols, because their meaning had been lost to the medal company, and to everyone else I knew. Probably, it was the symbol of the Essenes.

When God appeared to Abraham to announce the coming conception of Isaac by Sarah, he appeared as three persons. He did so to the confusion of Abraham and Sarah who were thoroughly ingrained with the belief in God's oneness. He was having his joke. He had Abraham rolling in the sand and had Sarah breaking her queenly decorum. He named the coming patriarch, Laughter, the translation of his Hebrew name. Thus God demonstrated that His oneness was not such that He could not appear as more than one when He wished.

After much thought, I have developed a concept of God, which is probably incorrect, but it works for me.

Since all matter and energy were indestructible, God was the indestructible end and the uncreated beginning. This is expressed in the formula: God= $I\infty$ $E\infty$

Where I= intelligence and E= energy. Infinite intelligence and infinite energy can do whatever it wishes. We are simply too simple to comprehend God. That is why He has given a revelation of Himself, to help us poor mortals who aspire to immortality.

Where for many years I had had personal experiences, now I felt obligated to go to the Jesuits and express them. But, which Jesuit? I had to be careful. I needed one who believed in God, His ability and the possibility of Revelation to a Jew. Someone who would listen: a saint.

Chapter Four

SHIRLEY

Every married man, and I am no exception, will admit that his life and what he has accomplished is most considerably due to his wife. Mine is Shirley Mae Fox. We met in November of 1946 as a result of a "blind" date. We were encouraged, harassed, and otherwise pushed into a meeting neither of us wanted. We had previously had unpleasant experiences.

A very close friend of Shirley's, Mr. Jerry Hirsch, married a very close friend of mine, Sylvia Bickoff. We both appreciated and loved our friends to the point where I finally called Shirley and she accepted. I convinced her that the date was the only way to satisfy our friends and get them "off our mutual backs." We agreed to attend a movie, go out for a snack afterwards, then tell our friends thanks, but no thanks.

When I arrived and rang the doorbell, Shirley opened the door immediately. She stepped out into the gentle light of the porch and I fell in love at first sight. She was beautiful, charming, obviously loved and cared for by her family. She moved gracefully. I waited anxiously to hear her voice. It was mellow, with beautiful phraseology and gentleness. She wore a sheared beaver coat on that cold November night in St. Louis, Mo., so I couldn't at that moment tell you anything else. I assumed the rest was of the best. Lightning had struck a discouraged bachelor, who felt that he would never meet a girl he would love.

Much happened between November 29, 1946 and November 27, 1947, the day we married. And now, we have five children, nine grandchildren and a toy poodle named Charlie. So much happened to us after that Thanksgiving. Some of it will be told later. Some of it will be left to Shirley and others to tell.

Important to our story is how our marriage came about. Eleven days before our nuptial we had a spontaneous gathering of interns in and around our rooms in St. Mary's Hospital. Everyone was talking about his or her coming engagements or weddings. Obviously, I was not a participant. As the conversations continued, the men began to flow out of our cell, and I was left alone. I was overcome with a sense of loneliness I had never experienced. Lying on the bed gave me a direct view of a crucifix on the wall. I thought and spoke within myself, "If you want me to marry the girl (Shirley), fix it up."

Four days later, a dinner party was held for the interns and residents. The dean of the medical school, Father Alphonse Schwitalla, and all the heads of departments were present. During the dinner the conversation again turned to weddings and engagements. The two doctors sitting across the table were really deeply engrossed in the subject.

Suddenly, another doctor turned to me. With a smile I had never seen on his gentle loving face, this previously unassuming, modest, religious man said to me, "You are going to get married! You're going to get married! You are going to get married before he does!!!" The last statement was a shout that brought the attention of the entire room to focus on us. The doctor began to laugh as if he had just pulled a great joke on me. His loud and raucous behavior was like what you would expect in a cowboy movie picture in a bar scene. He swayed in his chair from left to right to such a degree it appeared that he would fall, but he did not. Then he gradually regained his composure, and returned to his normal self.

I believe that he was possessed, but not by an evil spirit, but by the person I had inwardly addressed a few days before.

Father Schwitalla looked at me in puzzlement. I indicated to him by sign and gesture that it was all right. Calm soon prevailed, and everyone returned to his or her previous conversations.

I thought I would speak to my friend about this, but the events that followed prevented me from doing so. Three days later, I proposed to Shirley. After some hesitation, she accepted. Four days later we were married in a religious ceremony at her home. A rabbi we knew married us. Shirley's music teacher supplied the appropriate musical ambiance. Thanksgiving dinner was served for over one hundred-twenty relatives and friends. Harry Eidelman, Shirley's brother-in-law, took pictures. Everything was perfect.

My brother Bob, my best man, saved the broken pieces of glass that resulted from my crushing a goblet ending the wedding ceremony. He handed the pieces to me in a napkin as we left the car to enter our hotel. He advised me that I had to put the pieces together that night before anything else could take place. I wondered if the joker was following me, or if my brother was trying to start a new tradition.

It was twenty-five years later that I got to talk to the doctor who predicted my marriage. He told me that he knew something had happened that night, but he did not know what. Further, he had become quite prominent in his field and had also experienced speaking in tongues. Apparently, he had something serious to say, because the Paulist Fathers were working with him. He had joined the Charismatic Catholic movement. He had always been a devout member of the Roman Catholic Church.

I had always, and still do, regard Shirley as a gift of God. I believe that something had to be on my genetic code to cause the reaction I had when I met her. It was planned. It was orchestrated. Thanks.

Years later, perhaps when our oldest daughter, Ellen, was three, she took the responsibility. She said that she was up in heaven trying to get us together so she could be born. Funny thing, it seemed she treated us as if she was the parent and we were the loved, albeit simple, offspring.

Chapter Five

JESUITS AND DOCTORS

When I had the dream directing me to the Jesuit order, I was deeply involved in Jewish organizational work. I was "going through the chairs" of B'nai Brith, and eventually became President of the Pacific Palisades chapter. I was a member of the University Synagogue, and a member of their Board of Education. I had been the founder of the St. Louis chapter of Masada, and a very politically active President of the Zionist joint youth groups. During the pre-state status of Israel, I had worked diligently for the refugees of Europe to have a homeland. As a reward I had become the recipient of a week at Brandeis Camp in New York State, shortly before I became an extern in Jefferson City, Missouri.

After the war of independence, which created Israel and the Arab refugee camps, I worked to help the Arab brothers and sisters as well. They had become the refugees. I was completely frustrated in my efforts directed through the U.N., because the Arabs saw only one solution. Military. So the only answer became war. I had hoped that education of the refugees, helping them become productive citizens of any state, plus instillation of peaceful ideals of the U.N. Charter, would solve the problem. However, the idea of simply destroying the infant, weak nation with overwhelming power was too seducing to overcome. As I understand it, the Arabs strongly believe, perhaps more so than most, that "what is written by God will be." However, they elected to go against the will of God and his pledge to Israel, and in doing so with great might and persistence, proved it to be God's will at this time. I still believe, and still try to unite the family of Abraham at the Altar to God as desired and directed by Moses. At this writing, I have reason to hope for success. "Sharing is better than suffering," I say. Instead of fighting for control of Israel, the family must learn to joyously and peacefully share God's gifts. It is that or face ultimately the nuclear holocaust their leaders pursue as the goal to be desired. Why?

Men call themselves Homo sapiens, the wise animal. What conceit. Look at our history. Men have proven themselves for thousands of years to be anything but wise. We are told that the fear of God is the beginning of wisdom. The answer by a large, influential part of our civilization and some of its leaders is that God is dead, or worse, He never was. It's all an accident of cosmic gas. Religion is for show and dough, not go.

The result is that we are without a director. Musicians not playing the same tune, not playing together, create a discordant sound of horrible effect. With an accepted score and a director they follow, the results can be beautiful. We need a director; God is the only acceptable one to all.

I did try to bring "Holy Order" out of the chaos threatening us. That is why this Jew had to enter into conversation with his brothers of the Roman Catholic Church.

We have discord. Into this discordant jumble appears a Saint in the form of an Italian Pope, whose spiritual beauty was obvious and captivated the world. An accident! It was not intended by anyone other than God. The "real Pope," who later followed John, was too young. God took advantage of this, and worked through John.

Pope John XXVI opened the window to empty out the stale air of the Roman Catholic Church. He had been inspired to do so while in a garden in the Vatican, and to everyone's surprise, and to the dismay of some, he called for Vatican II. Some blame him, not God, calling for II.

It was at this time that this Jesuit trained Jew became influenced by the Presence and received His revelation, if indeed that is what time will prove it to be, and contacted Father Parrish. I was not sure at that time of my mental state. I asked for Father Frank's opinion. I had spoken at the request of my Rabbi at St. Martin of Tours Church. (Perhaps my Jesuit training influenced him.) Father A. Murray was pastor there. In return, Father Frank Parrish spoke at University synagogue. I was very impressed by the high spiritual quality and mystical knowledge of this tall, handsome, intelligent Jesuit. He was also a humble Jesuit. I wrote to him and we met at Loyola University. At that time I had been given the explanation for the Trinity, which he liked. (It was simple enough for children, but adequate for scholars.)

We went through the church together, looking for the answer to the sacrifice without waste, without finding it. We parted but kept in touch. I have the encouraging prayerful letters from that time and the comments made to me for the next three plus decades that brought us from the time of strength of manhood to the illness and experiences of old age. Together, we sought Divine answers through the Presence. Without Father Parrish's support, I do not know what I would have done. The mental strain was nearly overwhelming. During this time, I met Dr. Edward Colbert, a psychiatrist and devout Roman Catholic, at the counter in the Rose Room at St. John's Hospital. Accident or planned, I know not. We became friends.

I shared my thoughts and beliefs with Dr. Colbert, and sought his guidance and advice. He introduced me to Rotary International and to the "Religious Underground" at the Emerald Book Store in Santa Monica. He advised me and had me take a course in parapsychology at the University of California, Los Angeles. Here I met Dr. Thelma Moss, an expert in parapsychology. In her class, my ability to receive non-human transmitted messages was confirmed. I ignored human transmissions and received hidden transmissions five out of five times. Later, I was investigated in her laboratory in the presence of others including a student from behind the Iron Curtain, Czechoslovakia. She stated that to her knowledge, there were but two people in the world, myself included, who demonstrated this ability to "self-hypnotize." I demonstrated "going through the tunnel" as in the "near death experience," and brought back a message of caution for one of her students; her adventures into the occult were "dangerous to her soul."

Through Dr. Colbert and Father Parrish, I learned and progressed through the religious, medical, and social community. I had Father Parrish to keep me on the spiritual path. Dr. Colbert gave me assurance of psychological stability. Shirley, all else.

Father's first question was, "How will the Russians be conquered?" In a dream I saw God as a Russian farmer in control of the crops. I responded that He would conquer by controlling the farms and food production of the Soviet Union.

The next question I recall was, "When will it start?" In a dream I saw a toy store in Poland, and I entered it to find they were selling toy fisherman sets. Obviously, to God, it is a game played by His children.

He asked me for information that would confirm my statements; information which could not be obtained by normal methods. I read a newspaper article shortly after that time about Pope John having a problem with digestion. I had a dream that the saintly John had died, and I saw the new Pope. In the dream a voice said, "He has a blood-line claim to the throne." I told Father Parrish that the Pope would die, probably within nine months and the new Pope would be a scholar, but as tough as a tiger. I described him as pale, thin and bold. At Dr. Mack's office, in our coffee room, I picked the Pope-to-be out of those proposed for the position as stated in a newspaper article. My friend and fellow golfer, Henry Grisham, complained that I had picked the favorite. I told him that I picked the man I saw, and added that when did the favorite ever win? He answered, "That's right." I put my mission on the line. Later I learned that Pope Pius considered him like a son. In addition, his family was extremely powerful and supportive of the Roman Catholic Church. I believe that is what the "bloodline claim to the throne" meant.

What about private dreams? Shirley wanted to have a second home and decided she wanted one in Malibu. We looked at every home for sale in that area, yet did not find one to our liking. After looking a long time, I suggested buying a lot and building a home. In a dream, I saw myself in a ground level room looking out at my grandchildren playing in a lot that overlooked the Pacific Ocean. Trees surrounded it, but the slope of the hill permitted a beautiful view of the water. I told my family of the dream that concluded by my turning my head one-hundred-eighty degrees and going out through an odd-shaped window, meeting my departed Father Schwitalla, Dean of the medical school, and starting up a dark tunnel. That weekend we went lot hunting. The first salesman we met said, "Funny thing, a lot just came on the market. I would buy it myself, if I had the money." I described it to him. He asked me if I had been there. "How could I?" I replied. (In my dreams.) Shirley set the price at what she believed fair. When he attempted to bargain for the owner as becomes an agent, I stood behind the offer to test the validity of the dream. We got the property, at our price.

In the early sixties, shortly after teaching a Comparative Religion class at Loyola University, I wrote the pamphlet, "The Holy Order." In February 1966, upon suggestion by Dr. Colbert, I presented the lecture, "Evolutionary Religion," to the Catholic Physicians Guild.

I suggested the creation of a new order, a "Holy Order." It would be composed of people who wished to study God. Anyone who truly wished to know if God exists, communicates, saves, and loves us is in the Holy Order. It is a purely spiritual and intellectual pursuit of knowledge. The members of the Order may belong to any church or group. They may be of any race, sex, color, creed, or conviction. They have in common the desire to know. Hopefully knowing, they would follow the actions dictated by this knowledge. However, it would be rare that anyone could maintain perfection in this moral action. So we hope for the best type of moral action, but realize with Ben Franklin, that perfection is not attainable by men or women. I started the discussions with the story of an ancient Rabbi noted for his disbelief of the Torah, the five books of Moses.

A young man came to him and asked if he could become a great doubter like he was. The Rabbi asked the young man who Moses was. "Moses is the shopkeeper down the street," he replied. "And Abraham?" "Abraham is the old shepherd," he answered. "Moses is the lawgiver, and Abraham is the father of our religion and family. Go to school. Study. Then, when you know what to doubt, I'll teach you to doubt properly," pronounced the Rabbi.

Ignorance is not acceptable. A person must study to lift himself above his animal nature. Those who believe may one day disbelieve. Those doubting may be brought to belief. Certainly, ignorance is not disbelief. Learned disbelief is not only accepted, it is not uncommon.

A close friend of mine, who taught religion, renounced all his beliefs after losing his wife, and son. He had regained much materially and emotionally; but it had to be pointed out to him that, like Job, he was being tested.

I like to think of religion as climbing a mountain. One starts at the bottom and climbs up. As one climbs it becomes more difficult. One may stop, rest, and enjoy the life at any point in the climb. The higher you climb, the greater the risk of a fall, and the more dangerous. More is required as you reach levels where the air is thin, where the climber requires faith rather than logic.

On the first level we have atheism and polytheism. People believe in no God or many Gods. If a person denies a belief in God, to what does he dedicate his life? Does he pursue drink or drugs? Bacchus, God of wine? Sex? Venus? Power? Zeus? He shows by action what he truly loves. So a person claiming to be an Atheist may truly be the faithful worshiper of an ancient God, although he may not know or admit it. Abraham is given credit for coming to the belief in one God. As a child I was told that Abraham's father was a maker of idols. He left Abraham one day in charge of his store. Abraham smashed all the smaller idols and placed the hammer in the stony arms of the largest god. When his father returned, he asked Abraham what he had done. Abraham said that the large idol had done the deed. "That's impossible," replied his angry dad, "The idol has no power!" "Then why do you worship him?" replied his logical son. The Bible speaks of God revealing Himself to Abraham. Josephus writes of his logic telling him after observing the sea, wind, trees, and plants all responding together that only one God could obtain such complete harmony.

Logic tells us that since matter cannot be created or destroyed, it must have always been, and always will be. Since all things must have a cause, we must logically come to the conclusion that there was a first cause, now scientifically referred to as the "Big Bang." We come to the logical conclusion that the Big Bang had no previous cause; it always was and always will be, but it constantly changes to our senses. Water, snow, ice and back to water again. Water to hydrogen, to oxygen to explosion with liberation of energy, to water again. Constantly changing and returning.

God met Abraham and Sarah. He appeared as three persons. Sarah objected to Abraham, "You told me that He was one." God told Abraham that Sarah, in her old age, would conceive a son. Abraham fell down laughing; he, in his old age and Sarah so long barren! Sarah laughed quietly. God confronted her and said, "You laughed." "No, Lord," she modestly lied so as not to offend. Un-

offended the Lord answered, "You shall name the child, Laughter."
Isaac (which means laughter) was His little joke as well as a gift to
the couple. Isaac and his descendants were to become messengers
of their Creator and also a "litmus test" to the non-Jewish peoples.
Angry at God? Attack a Jew! Angry at morals? The Lord is not
fooled. He knows what is really being attacked, and what ancient
rebellious God (if any) the attacker truly worships, in the most
meaningful way, by imitation. The test shows the true nature of the
attacker.

The history of the attackers of the God of Abraham is not a
happy one.

It is unhappy for the Jews, but it results in a stronger people.
It is unhappy for others, because of their God.

Nature is infinite and beyond comprehension. It is put
together with infinite intelligence. So I believe that God is
infinitely intelligent and has infinite energy. This is convertible to
mass. God is expressed as God= $I\infty$ $E\infty$, where I is intelligence and
E is energy. Having reached the belief that there is a God, one
God, the next question is, does he communicate with man? The
stories of the Bible tell us He does. Do we have to believe them?
Are there reasons to believe them?

Josephus writes that from Abraham forward, the history of
the Jews is literally found in the Bible. The Bible is the source of
literature, law, medicine, military technique, and much more. In all
these things, and in historical fact, the Bible is wonderfully correct.
If it is correct in these things, then it follows that its main message
is correct: God is, and communicates with man.

It may seem difficult for you to believe God communicates. For
me it is a simple fact. The first time I spoke to God and was answered
was on a mountain in the Ozarks. At about fifteen years of age,
having to witness two boy scouts insist on fighting, and having served
as referee, I left camp to ask why this stupidity among men existed. I
found a rock that invited my knees, and knelt upon it. After about
twenty minutes, I received an answer. "Get up and go." I did, thinking
it a poor answer, and discovered my scout leaders were considering
sending out search parties to find me. After that, in school, church,
synagogue, car, in dreams, when it suited Him I would get a message.
I believe anyone can, if they take time to listen.

It was promised that if we ask we should receive. Certainly this meant spiritual gifts. What father, when asked to communicate with his child, by his child, would refuse? We know the story of the King, whose estranged son was far from him and wanted to see his father. When his son's friend asked the King to meet his son, the King replied, "Let him take the first step, and I shall take all the rest." So it is with God. Take the first step and wait, he will be there. The Bible, and the history of the nations, substantiates His communication. But personal contact is needed by many of us, not faith that someone else had contact. So, go for it yourself. Ask and you shall receive.

The next level on the mountain is the question of Jesus of Nazareth. Is he the Messiah promised to us by the Prophets? The entire New Testament and countless lectures, books, articles, and movies concern themselves with this man. Again, the literature is filled with pro and con arguments. It will come down to choice.

Josephus, in his history of the Jews, states that Jesus was the Messiah. However, it is argued that Josephus was edited and that was inserted. Then you have the deaths of those who followed him, because of his teaching. They, like Socrates, gave up their lives for truth. And you will have others saying, "What is truth?" In my case it came down to a personal matter. The voice of God within asked why I did not "cure" cancer before doing other studies. The Presence without, agreed that as a proof of His Messianic status, the drug Lysozyme would work in treating cancer. It did. No one else may believe it, but it did. Therefore, I am obligated to believe that Jesus of Nazareth is the Messiah, unless someone honestly proves me wrong. Nobody has even bothered to try, but an entire government has agreed to stop others and me from trying. If you wish personal contact, and ask for it, you shall receive it. It's the Messiah's promise.

I was told that the old Essene group of Jews still exists, and that they believe Jesus is the Messiah. A member of the Israeli Army told me that the Cabalists now believe it and are looking for a second Messiah to come. It's a certainty that many Jews believed it and were willing to die for that belief at the hands of the Romans. There are many logical reasons to believe, and there is faith.

Chapter Six

THE TRINITY

After explaining the Trinity, the virgin birth, the joyful and sorrowful mysteries, I considered the Roman Catholic Church obligated by its own dogma, to accept what I had explained. Added to this, the sign of the hand, and the many predictions which have all come true, I feel that the Vatican has gone back on its words. They, who condemned the innocent Hebrews to centuries of persecution and murder, have themselves refused to believe that which their own dogma insists can only come from God.

The Trinity explanation given above shall be repeated for clarity's sake. A circle represents God. A diameter of the circle represents the Holy Spirit, the Schkena of the Hebrews, spanning the Universe. A radius, perpendicular to the diameter, represents the Messiah, and the law of the universe. This represents the Universe under the law promulgated by the Messiah. If any element of this symbol is removed, its meaning is lost, but a new meaning is present. A circle, dash, numeral 1, a T, the Diner's club symbol, a rifle sight, all elements that can stand on their own. Together they form a single unit, a symbol. That is what I see God as being, a compound whose formula is $I\infty$ $E\infty$, infinite intelligence and infinite energy, which means it can also become matter in an intelligent form.

Another way to consider the unity is by example of the singleness of sugar. It is certainly a unique oneness; but sugar is composed of three elements: hydrogen, oxygen, and carbon. Put together with intelligence and energy, these two gasses and a black solid form a white sweet compound, which is a source of energy.

Genesis chapter eighteen tells of God appearing to Abraham and Sarah as three men. Why? I believe, to show that He would one day be called the Holy Trinity, yet be only one God with one will and one law. He made Abraham and Sarah laugh that day with His manner and His message. He named Abraham's son Isaac, laughter, so no one would forget His humor. We must remember our God as one who could appear as three. He promised to Abraham of the offspring Isaac, "All nations of the earth shall be blessed in Him."

He has set conditions. One, we must worship Him as He requires. Two, we make a sacrifice of belief that we know better how to conduct our lives than He, a sacrifice requiring an admission of our inferiority. It costs nothing. Pride has no value. (Try to buy a meal with it.) Yet our pride is a real sacrifice, difficult to make. That is the laugh; there is no waste; yet the gift leads to our happiness. Then we can do as He has ordered, LOVE ONE ANOTHER AS HE DID. That is, to the death. We have His promise of heaven after that, and the best possible life on earth.

The explanation of the birth of a child to a virgin came to me in a dream. I saw a form in a golden glow, to me it represented a failure of the egg in the reduction division phase to completely separate (who has not seen two un-separated seeds?). Then, by a small chemical change on the X chromosome to a Y1, the two eggs would become chemically different and unite to form a single egg with an XY1 chromosome. This would give us an unusual male. Why? It was believed that this form of birth was necessary to give Him the ability to understand women and be able to resist them. This could all be accomplished by a simple mutation.

Other mysteries, the Mona Lisa's smile, a form of malignant glaucoma, a treatment for cancer and possibly AIDS were all given to me and have been explained to many, and will be again at the appropriate time.

My pamphlet, "The Holy Order," suggested the re-creation of the Essene Order in a new form. Imagine a universal spiritual church, not requesting money, or control, or violence, presenting the word of God and letting mankind individually accept or reject that word, and taking the consequences of that action. In 1964, two people presented themselves to me as Essenes, informing me the Order was still in existence and functioning. On a return visit in 1989, they informed me the Order believed what I had said, to be truly from God. The same is true for many other people who have had many years to think about it. The Holy Order exists in the heart of many and hopefully it will make a difference to God.

Chapter Seven

THE HOLY ORDER

(As written in 1964)

INTRODUCTION

What do you want of life, health, and happiness? Physical and mental well - being are the sought after prizes. When we seek wealth, we believe it will make us happy and secure. When we seek the doctor from the day of birth through the day of death, we seek health.

Since the age of four, I have sought to improve myself so that I could bring health to people. I have become a doctor in pursuit of an honorable profession, and have done my best in this endeavor since 1947, until the present 1964. I have been richly rewarded for my efforts, and I hope I have helped others.

Now I wish to offer to you, mental well-being, and happiness. True, it will only be a small amount of your total need. Many other needs must be filled. But please permit me to offer this to you in the hope that you will derive a bit of happiness from it, and find a way to more.

LEVEL I

Long ago, before the Christian era, there was a group of Jewish people known as the Essenes. They separated themselves from the politics and strife of their day, to live quietly in communal settlements where they shared their labors and their rewards.

They believed in baptism as an act of purification. They believed in honesty and kindness and gave of themselves and their goods to others.

Some married and had children, some did not. Some went about like John the Baptist trying to elevate the morality of the people. Some remained quietly separating weeds from wheat.

They quietly awaited the Savior promised by the prophets; and when Rabbi Jeshua of Nazareth came and survived the crucifixion, many accepted Him as the Messiah. We are told that these wonderful people, called saints in their time, were the first "Christians."

Their order is no longer visible. Let us recreate it to the best of our ability. An order for Jew, Protestant, Catholic, Buddhist, Mohammedan, and yes, Atheist and Communist who wish to honestly seek God. All may join. It is a spiritual brotherhood without Church and clergy. All men and women in it are merely asked to seek truth and live according to their good conscience and the laws of their country.

LEVEL II

An Essene may go through four stages of mental attitude and development, or may remain at any attitude he wishes. He may join any church he desires or may belong to any Church.

The first stage of the order is for the Atheist who is willing to take a scientific attitude and seek God. All that is required is something along this line:

"God, if you do exist, show me and I shall follow. After all, if You exist, You are the wiser of the two of us and You should show me."

We shall symbolize this stage with a square of blue. This is the ancient Hebraic representation of the heavens, and merely indicates the face looking to the heavens.

The second stage of the Essenic Order indicates that the member has come to believe in God. This is symbolized by a white circle on the blue background. A circle is a sign which came long before the Hebrews. A circle has no beginning and no end. It may be infinitely large and curved like space. It includes all that is, and excludes all that is not.

As a guide to the second stage, the following suggestions are made:

God is the beginning. Everything that exists has a beginning and a cause, and that cause is capable of producing it. At the very beginning there must have been something that was without previous cause. How can that be?

Science says that it is a fact. Matter and energy can neither be created nor destroyed. If it cannot be created nor destroyed, it must have always been and will always be. That is what we say God is… the uncreated beginning and the indestructible end.

Spinoza eloquently tells of God and Nature being one. He tells of moral behavior based on logic. Good behavior must always be scientifically correct for the individual, the group and the natural law.

Einstein tells us that the universe is so complex, infinitely well-timed and put together that it is unscientific to assume it to be accidental. Rather, an infinite intelligence must have created it.

Spinoza with logic and Einstein with mathematics, found God to be infinitely intelligent. Einstein's theory of the oneness of matter and energy would permit us to say that God was infinite energy. Then God is Nature and God is infinitely intelligent. This intelligence has at its command, infinite energy.

We know that Nature (or God) has these qualities by our own observations.

LEVEL III

When we mention God, we have the connotation of a being interested in individuals. This brings us to the consideration of the third stage of the Essenes, which is that which believes that God communicates with man. This process is called prophecy and those men who act as messengers are called prophets.

This stage is symbolized by a diameter of the circle. This represents the spirit of God spanning the universe.

Dr. Richard Bucke, M.D. in his book, "Cosmic Consciousness," deals with the prophet from the point of view of the psychiatrist. Dr. Bucke believes that prophets are the result of evolutionary development and that they have attained a more advanced state of man. They have developed a sixth sense which communicates with God.

We study this field scientifically under the term "extra sensory perception." There is no doubt that it exists and it exists in different degrees in different persons.

When we believe that God uses this sense to communicate with certain individuals, we believe in prophecy.

The story of the Bible is the story of such men. The signs of the prophets are:

1. The ability to predict the future.
2. Concern with moral behavior.
3. Concern with physical well being.
4. Miracles, that is, knowledge and abilities to understand and deal with nature far surpassing other men of their time. A prophet may possess one or more of these abilities in a greater or lesser degree, but always to a greater degree than normal men of his time.

LEVEL IV

The fourth stage of the order believes, in the ultimate, in the fulfillment of the prophecies. They believe that the Messiah has come and that Rabbi Jeshua of Nazareth, Jesus Christ, was he.

This stage is symbolized by drawing a radius perpendicular to our diameter. The figure thus produces, represents the universe under the law of the cross.

The symbol has three distinct elements, yet is a single unit. As this is a unit, so these Essenes believe in the unity of the Father, Son and Holy Ghost thus represented...three elements of the one God.

All of us who seek God, or believe in God, or believe in prophecy or believe that the Christ has come, may be joined in one order. Together we can seek to bring peace to the world by putting our belief into action, beginning righteousness with ourselves and respecting others.

If the order exists within you, you are in the order. When it exists within everyone, we are close to brotherhood. When we put our beliefs into action, we have created the Kingdom of God on Earth.

Chapter Eight

GODTEMPLATION

All of nature's creatures seek material needs. Plants seek water with their roots, and light with leaves. Animals seek food, shelter, and mates. Man is a creature who also seeks to satisfy these needs. But man is not satisfied by material alone. Solomon with all his wisdom, wives, wine, and wealth, did not find happiness or contentment in things.

Man today, as Solomon yesterday, is unhappy with material alone. Why? Because material things decay and degenerate, and once men have satisfied the desire for them, their constant breakdown becomes an aggravation. More, they remind their owner of his own physical and mental changes. Material gains become burdensome physically and mentally.

Animals seem to know the extent of their need and stop gathering things, or are stopped by others or circumstances. Man can be insatiable, laboring night and day far in excess of his need, unhappy slave to desire.

As mankind is reminded by ageing of his approaching end, this scrambling becomes senseless. What has he missed? God. Man is different from all other animals. Man needs to know God personally or vicariously. Unless this need is filled, he has a void, which he mistakenly tries to fill with other things. Like a child eating everything to fill its stomach, man fills with material things to satisfy his hunger.

Hunger for God is never satisfied with things. Only God can fill that need properly.

How does man find God? Man is so accustomed to fighting and working for things that he assumes he must fight his way to God. Man has been willing to sacrifice anything to achieve the satisfaction of God hunger. God is not achieved. God is freely given to you if you freely give yourself. You give time and yourself, God, in His justice, will return at least equally of Himself.

Sit quietly, comfortably, and after study or preparation, wait for God to come, He shall. We cannot reach Him, as He can reach us. Let God come to you.

Invite Him in. Make your mind a quiet place, where inner sounds, inner pictures, and inner ideas can be experienced. Make your mind like a freshly washed blackboard and ask God to write thereon. Give Him time. God will do the rest. That is Godtemplation.

You will become aware of His presence, His voice, and His manifestations. Then you will never be God hungry again, and you will have God as your companion in all the trials of life.

Chapter Nine

SEEDS OF PEACE

When discussing political systems, arguments are filled with emotion. When speaking of automobiles, the conversation is generally amiable. These two systems, the first transportation, the second governmental, have much in common. All automobiles available on the market can get you from one place to another. The most deadly thing about them is the driver. Most political systems can function adequately; it is the people who run the system who make it a blessing or a disaster. The need is more for people improvement than system change, though systems should be constantly improved also.

Wars between political systems can be compared to accidents between automobiles. If the rules of the road are obeyed, there are fewer accidents. Staying in your own lane can be compared to staying in your own space. As auto accidents (which are space confrontations) frequently involve the innocent, so do wars.

What really matters are careful drivers, who keep their autos in safe condition, and who drive with courtesy, and intelligence. The same is required of political leaders. We can learn the way of peace every day, on the highways. We can see the war makers. The truth is that more deaths occur on American highways than on American battlefields. It is the same aggressive act at work.

What is needed is a method of testing for leaders of both systems, both political and transportation. Drivers have to take comprehensive tests, physical, mental, and intelligence. If they fail, they are not allowed to drive. This is usually peacefully achieved and no one is offended. If time proves they are bad drivers, they lose their license. Should we do less with political leaders who can destroy the planet? They should be peacefully removed from office as well.

Whatever the political system and transport system, it is up to individuals to bring peace to the world. Starting with you, drive carefully, and function politically with care.

How do we learn care? One way is to plant seeds of trees, and watch the "Seeds of Peace" grow. Learning the care, information and patience necessary for this project is an education. The sum total is a gain in wisdom and grace, and an appreciation for what we have in nature. Hopefully, we will learn the effort, and care needed to grow something, and thus hesitate to destroy it. In addition, we have added immeasurably to the environment.

If one believes in God, one believes that only with the Creator's help can such a Spiritual-Intellectual awakening occur in Man. We have the Word that one day each man will sit under his own tree in peace. We are preparing for that day by bringing in "Seeds of Peace" from the Holy Land and raising these trees toward that time. We hope you join us.

Chapter Ten

CHILDREN OR NOT

"If I'd have known grandchildren were so much fun, I'd have had them first." I first heard this from Shirley. Now, she wears it on her T-shirt.

Nature has placed within us strong rewards for having and properly raising children. In past societies, children were a worker's security in old age, cheap labor, and protectors in time of war. Now they are expected to go to school until the age of eighteen. This means a long time of financial dependency on the parents and the community. They are a long time burden for a distant return.

The first emotion I felt looking at my newborn daughter was a tender, heart-tugging love. The second was as if a heavy load was placed on my shoulders; I almost bent under its weight. Within me, my own inner self said, "This is your responsibility."

When my first granddaughter, the most beautiful child I had ever seen, was presented, the emotion was entirely different. I wanted to go to the top of the roof and "crow" like a rooster at sunrise. Her father had somehow become more heroic in appearance to me. We enjoyed a friendly relationship, but now I saw what a charming fellow he was. I really loved him.

I have never heard of anyone being proud of an abortion. I have never seen anyone show pictures of their aborted fetus. No congratulations, no showing, only depression, sadness, guilt, and regret.

What causes abortions? Many causes are given for the fetus being unwanted. Rape and incest are the most often mentioned. The inability to raise the child, career, and financial stress, political, overpopulation reasons; FEAR, FEAR, FEAR.

What are the types of abortions? Legally, there are criminal and non-criminal abortions, depending on the laws of the state. Medically, there are surgical and pharmacological abortions.

I have listened to the arguments on both sides; finally, I prayed for an answer. What is the teaching of the conscience within? I had a dream that cut through pure logic.

My son and I were on a deer hunt. The lives of the entire family depended upon the result of the hunt. We were starving, and this would be the last hunt we could make. My son suggested that we separate in order to cover more ground. I agreed. About an hour and a half later, I heard or sensed a noise in the bushes. I turned to see a form, but I could not determine what it was. It was sunset. The lighting in the dense forest was poor. The form was close. The question was: Do I fire?

I have told the story to many people. Some say they would shoot and some say not. The reason for not shooting is that they do not know what was in the bush. Some would face the certainty of loss of the entire family. If I did fire the shot, and thus accidentally killed my son, would the family regard what I brought back from the hunt as meat, rather than my son?

Some time later a Jesuit came to lecture at St. John's Hospital on the subject of ethics. At the break, Dr. Edward Colbert and I were sitting by his side. After he answered a few questions from other doctors, I told him about the dream. After laughing a bit, he answered us that he had done his doctorate on this problem, which he said is a classic problem in ethics. I asked him what his conclusion was. He remained silent. I pressed him for an answer. He remained silent. Again and again, I asked. He relented and answered that he felt to shoot would be a "justifiable risk". So he had stated in his doctorate.

The basic issue is what is in the pregnant womb. Is it part of the mother over which she has complete authority? Or is it a human being with rights of its own? There is no way of our knowing at this time in a scientific way. Who can prove the existence of a soul? Or when the soul enters the body? One religion may say that it is part of the mother until the umbilical cord is severed. Others may contend that the child has a soul of its own from the moment the sperm enters the egg. When is that? What is in the bush? What is in the womb? Who can prove it?

Religious arguments should remain just that. Arguments. Jumping up and down. Yelling! Screaming! No hitting! Blows only show who is more powerful, not who is correct. After a while those who yell and scream and jump up and down tire of this display. Then they can be more rational and discuss the matter. Certainly there is no scientific answer, so my dreams are as good as the next person's. At least, they are to me. It was I who held the gun. It was I who bore the pain. It is I who will answer to God! Why are you jumping up and down? Cannot a just and merciful God who put me in this position judge me?

I am sixty-eight years old at this writing. Almost all the writing to this section has been aboard aircraft from zero to thirty thousand feet. I have passed through and around thunderstorms with a display of lightning that cannot be believed unless seen. One person on the ground was struck in the head and killed. I have seen clearly, as if viewing from high above on a cloud. I have seen from the ground to as high as a commercial airplane goes on this route. Bumpy air and clear.

I have recently experienced the pain of which is said to be comparable to a woman having a child. Nature can inflict pain and fear and mental anguish beyond your power to believe unless you have experienced it. God, or Nature, doesn't need mankind to inflict pain. Has not Nature planted within most of us a conscience to guide? Under conditions where we cannot know what the truth is, we must trust the individual conscience.

In 1978, I was privileged to go to China as part of a goodwill tour. Shirley and I went to Hawaii around 1976 and discussed a trip to Mainland China. She wanted to go because of her interest in copper enameling. I wanted to go because I wished to speak to someone there who could convey what I thought and felt to the government. We had fought two wars against the Chinese in Korea and Vietnam. I saw no reason for it all. We are not natural enemies; we have everything to gain in friendship.

On my trip to China I was shocked by the love the Chinese showered on their children. At that time, the children were dressed in brightly colored clothing. They were kissed, hugged, pushed like royalty in carts. They were carried with pride and affection. They are the future of the parents.

Yet, in this country, families are limited in size to one or two children. Abortion is a national policy. Why? Because the Chinese know war and starvation, and a large population means both. War in a nuclear age has entirely different meaning than previously. China cannot invade without risking the good earth as well as its military. It can get more people; but if the ground is radioactive and vegetation destroyed, disease and starvation are right behind. You may mentally convict them, not I.

Judge not least you be judged.

Let he who is without sin cast the first stone.

Love one another as I have loved you (to the death).

The story of the adulterous woman and the orders of the world's most famous itinerant carpenter command us to permit personal freedom on the part of our brothers and sisters.

If you do not want the fetus killed, make it possible for the woman to have the child. Do what you can to help her, if you wish. To physically attack her is contra-productive. If you can break the law violently, why shouldn't someone else do likewise? Why not she?

Hitler pointed to the violent acts of the Church, and so justified his own violence. The end does not justify the means. The means, love, is also the end. How can the Church and Christians not try to win with love?

Chapter Eleven

BIRTH CONTROL

Shirley and I have five living children. We lost one, a beautiful baby boy, who died in utero. As the doctor and Shirley would have it, I delivered the baby. It would be unpleasant and unnecessary to give the details except those essential to the story.

For a brief period following the delivery, Shirley became pulse-less. I was left in a situation where my child had become a medical specimen for study, my wife appeared dead, and I was to be left with five small children to raise without my wife. At that time, for these circumstances, no medical alternatives were known nor recommended to me. Shortly, her pulse returned to normal.

Both Shirley and I agreed that we could not risk another pregnancy, even though we wanted another child. Birth control was the answer for us.

We did this because we wanted to be there for the children we had. I did not wish to risk losing my wife. Either reason, I believed, was adequate to justify my action. Yet some would condemn this action if artificial methods were used to prevent conception. How would they behave if they were in my position?

I had explained my position on birth control to my Jesuit brothers. They asked if I would study the matter and get back to them. I left to satisfy this question. I would have to have an argument against infallibility.

By this time my physician, Dr. Mack, had advised me to take up golf... too much work and no play. My wife had given me a starter golf set to lure me away from fishing, so I took it as a good sign. Why fight it? Two top authorities.

I started by getting some lessons from a golf pro who taught at a driving range in Westwood Village. He watched me swing and gave me the following advice, "Wear nice clothes and swing pretty. From the clubhouse nobody can see where the ball goes." I should have expected difficulties, he never bothered to teach me to aim, just fire away with a nice swing.

One day, while resting from religious experiences, and practicing my iron shots, I saw a vision. That is, I saw Rabbi Jeshua in the clouds with his Apostles sitting quietly behind him. Within myself, my first reaction was, "Not again." I had seen the vision first on hitting the ball into the sky. I looked down, then tentatively up again, "What is it, Lord?" I said within myself. He answered, "Take a club in both hands. Put two balls down, one on the right, another on the left, hit them both at the same time. One ball should go three hundred yards into the hole. The other ball should make circles around the first, and then go into the hole together." I looked down. "But Lord," I replied, "...that's impossible without a miracle."

He answered, "If you cannot do such a simple physical thing, where do you get off thinking you (man) can make moral laws?" He was gone when I looked up.

Father Parrish had asked me what I thought of birth control. I had told him. I also told him that I believed it came to the question of infallibility. Now, months later, I believed that I had the answer for him on infallibility.

God decides moral law. If God inspires a man, then he can be infallible by doing the Divine will. If not, man is a fallible being. And as far as God is concerned, we are as grains of sand on the beach to him. All perhaps different one from the other, yet all of approximately equal size and value. The Pope is Peter. Well, Peter had arguments with Paul, and lost. When he wanted to run away from Rome, Christ himself had to make him return to face crucifixion. Peter was not infallible. Neither is his successor. Nor is a prophet, if he strays from the Divine command. Remember how Jonah had to be placed on the right path. Once he had done his job, he had another disagreement with his boss, and had to be straightened out.

Man is just a man. Even if he has a high opinion of himself, and others have an even higher opinion, he is still, "a grain of sand on the beach" to God. His powers, mental and moral, are finite. So, God is the moral judge of acts.

Nor did the teaching of that day end with the vision. I had taken off my wedding ring and put it in my pocket. In my state of mind, I rushed to get my golf equipment together, and lost the ring in the grass on the driving range. I missed it when I got home, and informed the people there of my loss.

The ring was found by the person mowing the grass, and turned it in at the office. The office called and told me that the ring had been found when the bright glint of the gold was seen as the grass over it was cut. The ring was nicked somewhat by the mower, but otherwise was intact. I offered a reward to the people at the office for the groundskeeper. Oddly, they refused it with a polite sincere smile.

When I returned home, I told Shirley about the incident, and of their refusal to take a reward. We were both equally impressed with their behavior. I asked Shirley to take the ring to the jeweler and have it repaired. She did. It was repaired. The jeweler refused to take any payment for the work involved. Was the hand of God in this?

How strange? I really was upset about losing that ring. It had some actual value, but the sentimental value was very great. Did God also want a wedding ring? Did the Creator want a symbol between us? What would be an appropriate symbol? These questions and the answers to them were to occupy my mind for the next three decades.

The question of birth control itself was not settled with me by this revelation, infallibility was. It was by a strange spiritual marriage. After Father Parrish and I had discussed my beliefs on the birth control question, he asked me to try for a sign. He asked for confirmation as a Jesuit does. One night at about 8pm, I was leaving St. John's Hospital in Santa Monica. I had finished my visits to my patients. Within twenty-five steps from the door, a presence of Mary occurred above and behind me. "Where are you going?" asked the voice within. "I'm going home." "No, you're not. You are going to the chapel."

Why fight it? I couldn't win. So I went to what was soon to be destroyed, the small chapel in St. John's. I went the way of the "Rose Room" where we met in small groups for food and coffee, and food for thought. I was praying quietly in the dimly lit chapel when some Sisters came in and began reciting the rosary behind me. I wanted to leave, but I did not wish to walk through them. After a short time, I began to feel "lifted up" by their prayers. The spirit took hold of me. In my mind's eye I could see Christ before me. After a short time I had an ecstatic gut inner experience that could only be related to a wedding night. Then suddenly both my hands began to hurt. I thought that perhaps it was from gardening, using a hand shovel, especially on the right hand. While I was thinking this, He said within me, "Then I'll take the left." After a time, He left and the Sisters left. Slowly my hands returned to normal. He will take my hand? I was frightened. Will I lose my hand? Late I learned that He would hold my hand as I walked through life.

For a while after this experience, my hands would assume the appearance of a dead man's, blue and mottled. It would not last long, and it would precede an office visit from a religious person, or some event to which serious, though small, religious significance could be attached. After Father Parrish asked me about a sign to reinforce my position, I awoke knowing that I had the ability to control "the hand." I invited Father and a friend to the Wilshire Hilton for dinner. During dinner we excused ourselves briefly from Shirley, and I demonstrated to them what I called a mini-resurrection. First it looks dead, and then it's alive. Is that not what the Lord had done? Both Jesuits admitted to seeing the sign, but not to what I considered it meant. Nor did I ask them. I knew their responsibilities.

Later I met Father and another Jesuit at Loyola University. As I recall, they requested further signs. I replied that I was afraid to go for more since the resurrection was the basis for Christianity. That should be enough. It is a fearsome job. I would do it, but I wanted it in writing that if I produced, they would support my position.

Father Parrish left and the other Jesuit priest said to me, "Then this will be the sign, if you are right, the church will be destroyed. If the church is right, you will be destroyed." I did not completely accept that as the case. I answered, "God has nothing against the buildings and the beautiful artwork. What will be destroyed will be the teaching authority of the Church. It will be done slowly, to save from despair those innocents who cling to the

Church for support, and to give those responsible, time to change their minds." He nodded. And so it is and was.

I had a heart attack at age sixty-eight. God spared me with the swift hands of the paramedics, the new drugs, and angioplasty. I have been given time to write this book, to properly prepare to die, and God only knows what else. I have been a complete success by my standards. I've had a wonderful wife, life, children, grandchildren, adequate fame, adequate fun, and the best of everything. My cup runneth over. I got a bigger cup. It did the same.

I saw Pope Paul die fighting disgrace. I saw Pope John Paul I terminated. I saw Pope John Paul II almost terminated, but spared by God to be given a chance to do what needed to be done to save the church if he would, and start the final episode of the Soviet collapse.

One day at Saint John's we held a meeting of the Catholic Physicians' Guild. We had a speaker, Mr. Wayne Moye, who informed us that the Pope would go against the doctors and veto birth control using artificial means. At this meeting, I forwarded my prediction of the downfall of the Church as a teaching authority. Before the next meeting, the Pope issued his statement.

It was our group's policy to have mass before the Guild's meeting. There was only one lone person at mass besides the Jesuit priest. Myself. No one else attended the meeting. The Guild ceased to exist, and efforts to resurrect it failed. The Pope offended the doctors. The doctors offended the priest. The falling away had begun as predicted and in my own front yard.

But, I still had the sign, and though at first I was afraid to use it, I was later more afraid not to do so. One night after saying my "Now I lay me…" prayer, I decided not to use it again, even for teaching. I awoke with my right arm essentially "dead" from shoulder down. So much for telling the boss what to do, or what I would do. As I relented and pledged to obey, I received my right arm back. So literally hundreds of people have had this sign demonstrated.

What appears dead is not necessarily dead, if you have been given control. Thus by demonstration to doctors, professionals, priests, nuns and all who were interested, I have been able to show that the signs of death mean only clinical, not biological death. I've shown that a person can, by prayer and grace, appear dead and return to full function within minutes. Other mysteries like the virgin birth would also be explained in understandable terms.

So what does one do in this life to secure entrance into the Kingdom Heaven? You live as if God were your King while you are on earth. When the time comes that your spirit leaves your body, it has already achieved its passport into the Kingdom of Heaven. And what type of behavior is that? As Mothers tell their children, and my grandchild repeated to me, "Be Nice." Just be nice and love one another.

EPILOGUE

What has happened that is constructive as a result of the messages? According to Father Parrish, there are four hundred churches using the method of The Holy Order, as of 2004. Father Parrish used other teachings from mystical messages in articles he wrote concerning the Eucharist. Until a few months before his death, he continued to encourage me in my efforts, and confirmed his belief in the messages. As predicted to the Catholic Physicians Guild, the failure to follow the teachings given to them has led the Roman Catholic Church into a period of decline.

Lysozyme was found to be effective in some forms of cancer in the very late stages of the disease. The report of our investigations was made public to the entire scientific community. Laws passed that prevented doctors from using foreign drugs to treat patients, ended our experiments. However, I tried it on myself and arrested early cancer of the prostate for ten years. All efforts, local, state, national, and international, to have some other group pick up the study, failed. When the AIDS epidemic occurred, I suggested that lysozyme be tried as a treatment. It has been used in Europe for other viral diseases. All efforts to obtain permission to use lysozyme on this fatal disease failed. There is no rational basis for this attitude, but that is the way it has been in this country.

As I understand it, the U.S. government does not give patent rights on naturally occurring substances. (Lysozyme is found in nature in plants and animals. In our research, we used chicken egg white lysozyme.) It is noteworthy that this enzyme, lysozyme, was discovered by Alexander Fleming, M.D., the same doctor/scientist who discovered penicillin. We know the far reaching effect this has had on public health and further research! Lysozyme was discovered before penicillin.

At the scientific meeting in Milan, Italy in 1964, at which my paper and many others were delivered, I met Dr. Fleming's widow. She expressed to me that Dr. Fleming felt that lysozyme would become more effective in public health than penicillin, but that he did not know in what way. Dr. Fleming was a part-time scientist and a part-time practicing physician. He wanted his scientific research to be useful in helping people and preventing disease. He was a wonderful man. I was influenced by his actions.

I hope that lysozyme will be scientifically investigated and found to show useful results in the treatment of cancer and other diseases. Is it only that it is monetarily unprofitable and therefore untouched by pharmaceutical corporations?

Messages have been shared with other governments with the permission of the government of the USA. In Israel, there now exists the Peace Park, a place where all people can pray at the wall of the Old City. A stone has been erected in Kfar Gilade, upon which is written a prayer for peace. A grove of one thousand trees, The Universal Peace Grove, exists where the Messiah can rest. China and Russia are friendlier, and efforts are underway to do the same with the Arab Nations. Only time can say if our messages were helpful. With God, all things are possible.

This is the situation as of June 2012. I am 89 years old and in reasonably good health, enjoying the good life. The overwhelming majority of the Roman Catholic laymen have rejected the concepts of the Vatican regarding contraception. No one has disputed my revelations concerning the mysteries of the Church. I wish to thank the sisters and priests for their cooperation and for the assistance of many lay Catholics who have been kind and helpful to me. The Roman Catholic Church is in disgrace; the vast majority does not accept the words of the Pope.

I believe that we can all communicate with God. We can obey our good conscience. And I believe the basic rule of life, as taught to me by my three-year-old granddaughter is, "Be Nice."

CPSIA information can be obtained at www.ICGtesting.com
Printed in the USA
LVOW09s1236181114

414245LV00005B/224/P